Outside a storm was brewing.
Lucy helped Jamie finish
his painting, and then they
got ready for bed.

The wind rattled the windows.
Jamie hugged Floppy Rabbit,
as Dad read his
favourite book
to help him sleep.

But after Dad had gone, Jamie still couldn't sleep.
The wind howled outside and a rumble of thunder grew.
Jamie hugged Floppy Rabbit as tightly as he could.

"We should go somewhere where there is no thunder," whispered Lucy. "I think Turtle knows a place."

"With no thunder?" asked Jamie.

"With NO thunder!" said Turtle.

"Climb up on me and I'll take you there."

Jamie, Lucy, Bear, Foxy,
Tiger and Floppy Rabbit
went with Turtle, far, far away,
deep under the ocean.

"There's never any thunder here," said Turtle.
"That's why us turtles like it!"
"But I'm not a turtle, and I don't
want to live underwater!" cried Jamie.

"I know a better place," said Foxy,
and so Turtle swam on.

When they reached land, Jamie cried,
"It's thundering here, too!"

"But not in this tunnel. Follow me!" said Foxy,
and they ran down and down, deep into the earth,
and the sound of thunder faded.

"There's no thunder down here," said Foxy,
"that's why us foxes like it!"
"But I'm not a fox and I don't want
to live underground!" cried Jamie.
"I know the best place!" said Lucy.

And so they ran on.

"That's the best place. That's Fairy Castle,"
said Lucy. "Come on!" She grabbed Jamie's
hand and tugged him along the path.

Thunder rumbled all around them
as they ran up and up.

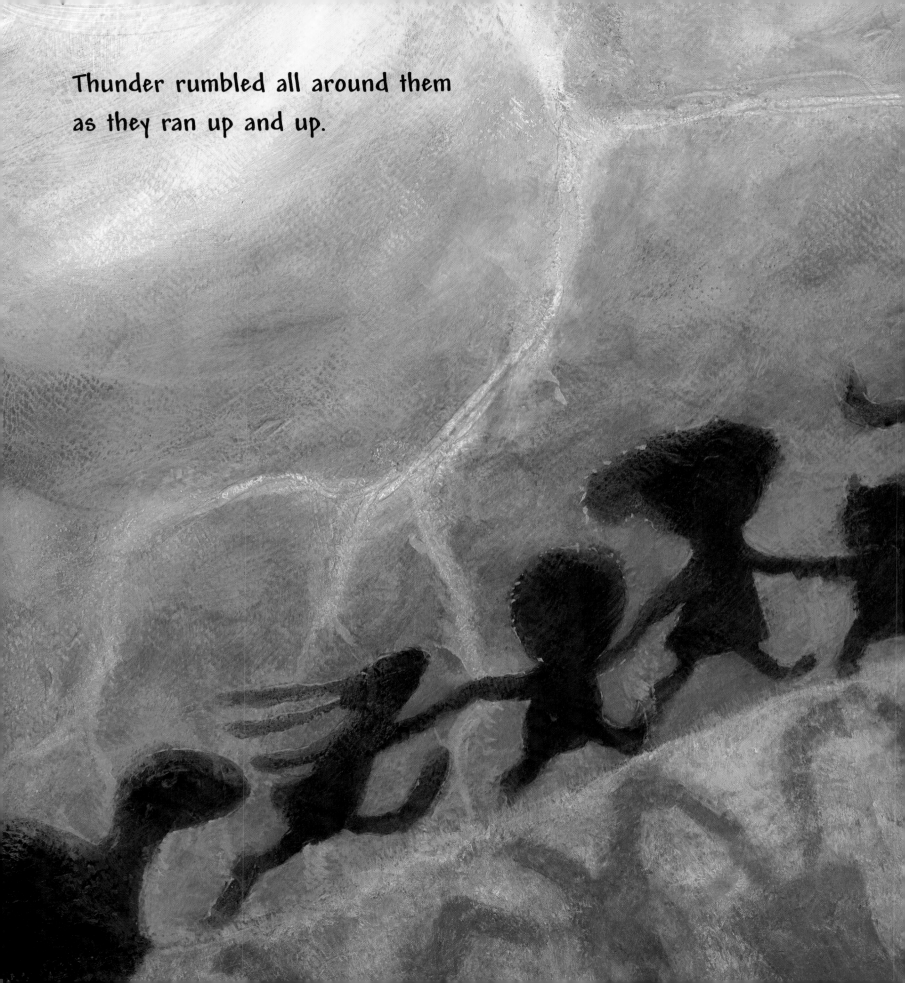

But the lightning cracked and the thunder rumbled
louder than ever.
Jamie stopped.
"I can't!" he cried. "I'm too scared!"
   "T . . . try and be brave," stuttered Tiger, trembling.
"All tigers are meant to be brave!"

"But I'm not a tiger and I don't want to be brave!" cried Jamie.

Lucy took hold of Jamie's hand.
"The fairies will help us make it stop," she said.

Jamie hugged Floppy Rabbit tighter than ever, took a deep breath,

and ran as fast as he could through the rain.

They reached the door.
"It's shut!" said Lucy,
pushing hard. "It's too big!"

"Everyone push!" shouted Jamie.
He threw himself forward
and they all pushed . . .

and pushed . . .

and slowly the huge door
began to creak open . . .

. . . and they tumbled into the light.
There were fairies everywhere!

"They're painting!" said Lucy.

"Help us magic the thunder away," said a fairy.

"I'm not a fairy," said Jamie, as he took the magic brush, "but I'll try!"

And try he did. Soon Jamie was splashing light and colour about . . .

following the fairies through the castle . . .

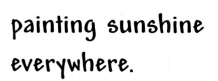

painting sunshine everywhere.

Up and up they went . . .

. . . up to the very heart of the storm.

Jamie swung his magic brush
up into the sky.

Colour and light leapt into the clouds, breaking them apart. Sunshine flooded across Fairyland and, at last, the thunder stopped rumbling.

Jamie, Lucy, Bear, Foxy, Tiger, Turtle

and Floppy Rabbit danced up and through the rainbow, all the way home . . .

"It's morning," said Lucy,
"and the thunder's gone!"
"I magicked it away!" said Jamie.
"I must be a fairy after all!"